Shadow Work Journal

Guided Prompts and Questions to Integrate Your Shadow, Release Emotional Blockages, and Express Your Authentic Self

© Copyright 2025 - All rights reserved.

The content contained within this book may not be reproduced, duplicated, or transmitted without direct written permission from the author or the publisher.

Under no circumstances will any blame or legal responsibility be held against the publisher or author for any damages, reparation, or monetary loss due to the information contained within this book, either directly or indirectly.

Legal Notice:

This book is copyright-protected. It is only for personal use. You cannot amend, distribute, sell, use, quote, or paraphrase any part of the content within this book without the consent of the author or publisher.

Disclaimer Notice:

Please note the information contained within this document is for educational and entertainment purposes only. All effort has been executed to present accurate, up-to-date, reliable, and complete information. No warranties of any kind are declared or implied. Readers acknowledge that the author is not engaging in the rendering of legal, financial, medical, or professional advice. The content within this book has been derived from various sources. Please consult a licensed professional before attempting any techniques outlined in this book.

By reading this document, the reader agrees that under no circumstances is the author responsible for any losses, direct or indirect, that are incurred as a result of the use of the information contained within this document, including, but not limited to, errors, omissions, or inaccuracies.

Your Free Gift
(only available for a limited time)

Thanks for getting this book! If you want to learn more about various spirituality topics, then join Mari Silva's community and get a free guided meditation MP3 for awakening your third eye. This guided meditation mp3 is designed to open and strengthen ones third eye so you can experience a higher state of consciousness. Simply visit the link below the image to get started.

https://spiritualityspot.com/meditation

Or, Scan the QR code!

Table of Contents

INTRODUCTION 1
SECTION 1: CONFRONTATION 3
   FACE YOUR SHADOW SELF 5
SECTION 2: ACCEPTANCE 23
   EMBRACE YOUR INNER WOUND 25
SECTION 3: RELEASE 49
   CAST AWAY LIMITING BELIEFS AND EMOTIONAL BLOCKAGES 51
SECTION 4: INTEGRATION 81
   MERGE WITH ALL PARTS OF YOU 83
SECTION 5: AUTHENTICITY 101
   STEP INTO YOUR TRUE SELF 103
CONCLUSION 119
HERE'S ANOTHER BOOK BY MARI SILVA THAT YOU MIGHT LIKE 122
YOUR FREE GIFT (ONLY AVAILABLE FOR A LIMITED TIME) 123
REFERENCES 124
IMAGE SOURCES 130

Introduction

No one is perfect. Everyone has an Achilles heel, makes mistakes, and suffers from emotional scars. All of these are part of being human. You can't go through life without negative emotions, unpleasant thoughts, or socially unacceptable desires. You deny these aspects of yourself, keeping them hidden, afraid of being judged or rejected for who you really are.

Denying certain aspects of your personality can damage your mental health, emotional health, and well-being. You need to accept and embrace every part of yourself. This can be done with shadow work.

Shadow work basically involves connecting with your unconscious mind to reveal your repressed personality so you can heal and fully accept yourself.

This book introduces the concept of the "Shadow Self" and the importance of acknowledging the hidden parts of yourself. It will help you come to terms with your darkness, accept yourself, and find emotional freedom.

Your darker side is the result of your trauma and pain. Your unhealed emotional wounds tend to eventually create a barrier when it comes to forgiving yourself and your past.

Most limiting beliefs can restrict your freedom and keep you from growing, meeting your goals, or realizing your true potential. This is why overcoming these thoughts and emotions will set you up to be who you have dreamed of being. You will be able to face your fears and self-doubt once you find what triggers them.

You can't truly recognize your strength if you've never acknowledged your weaknesses, just as you can't fully appreciate your light without having encountered darkness. Each person is a mix of highs and lows, filled with both defeats and victories. You can't just focus on one side and ignore the other; embracing all parts of your personality is essential for finding inner peace.

The final section of the book guides you in accepting your true self by aligning your actions and behaviors with your core values and beliefs. It encourages you to conquer your fears and break free from societal expectations, allowing you to lead a meaningful life without the weight of judgment or rejection. Plus, each chapter includes thoughtful journal prompts designed to help you reflect and gain a deeper understanding of yourself.

The Benefits of Reading Shadow Work Journal Book:
- Gaining a deeper understanding of shadow work and how it can bring awareness to repressed emotions and hidden beliefs
- Clarity in identifying emotional wounds and negative thought patterns
- A safe space to explore and release repressed emotions through guided prompts and creative expression
- The ability to integrate the shadow self and heal past trauma
- The creation of a consistent, mindful practice for personal growth

Section 1: CONFRONTATION

Face Your Shadow Self

Coming to terms with some of the more unsightly elements of your personality – like anger, sadness, or cruelty – is a challenge many people face. Most individuals choose to ignore these aspects of themselves and bury them deep within. The shadow self cannot be denied indefinitely. Concealed feelings, perceptions, and opinions will eventually manifest through crying or uncontrolled rage. To heal and grow, acceptance of these repressed aspects is the only way forward.

Identifying and facing your shadow self is the first step to healing.[1]

The purpose of this chapter is to describe your shadow self, enabling you to explore your hidden emotions, beliefs, and past memories with a set of prompts and questions.

What Is the Shadow Self?

Certain aspects of one's personality, including fears, emotions, and desires, are referred to as the *shadow self*. It is the version of yourself that you struggle to accept and is in deep slumber, so to speak. The majority of people suppress the traits that embarrass them or simply do not conform to societal expectations. A reflection of someone's shadow self is usually buried underneath. Acceptance and recognition of this aspect requires reflection and thoroughly comprehending your character.

The term "The Shadow" was first used by Swiss psychologist Carl Jung, who attributes it to the savage parts of an individual. In Jung's words, each individual possesses dual sides, including the persona that everyone can see, or in other words, one's public personality, and the shadow self, the concealed, sinister half that resides within.

Rather than perceiving the shadow self as a sinister side, Jung considered it a neutral component of a person that must be examined to attain a better grasp of one's self. To some degree, he claimed that it is impossible to uncover the shadow side without first understanding the persona. That is when a person can seize their irrational urges.

Suppressing your shadow self can have troubling consequences. You might experience a lack of self-worth, anxiety, depression, a holier-than-thou attitude, narcissism, self-defeat, difficulty forming relationships, being misleading, and harmful and aggressive behavior.

Your shadow self is extremely vital to understand because it is the most sensitive part of your personality. Particular circumstances can be motivational, or it can go the other way around – you might project self-doubt and blame your shortcomings on others. For instance, if you suppress sadness, you might look down on people who mourn openly or even go to the extreme of disciplining children for crying.

Never avoid or feel shame when it comes to your shadow self. It is something that calls for nurturing and healing. Accepting all dimensions of your personality can enable true emotional freedom, self-respect, and wholeness.

Shadow work allows you to tap into your unconscious to reveal and confront traumatic or undesirable patterns of your personality. It involves journaling, self-reflection, visualization, and other techniques to awaken self-awareness and self-acceptance.

Once you begin shadow work, you will start seeing your shadow self in a different light and learn to treat it with love and compassion.

Benefits of Shadow Work

- Boosting self-esteem
- Improving creativity
- Self-awareness
- Self-compassion
- Self-acceptance
- Feeling sympathetic towards other people's shadow selves
- Improving well-being

Prompts and Questions

This journaling section helps start the process of facing the shadow self. However, this is only the beginning of your journey.

Emotions that Feel "Too Much"

Reflect on your hidden or suppressed emotions, such as sadness, shame, or anger.

1. What emotions do you struggle with facing or expressing?

_____
_____
_____
_____
_____
_____
_____

2. Why can't you acknowledge and confront these emotions?

_____
_____
_____
_____
_____
_____
_____

3. What do these emotions need from you?

4. What do you usually feel when you experience overwhelming emotions?

5. When do you usually feel powerless and unable to control your emotions?

6. What emotions do you usually judge others for or project on them?

7. What parts of yourself do you keep from your loved ones?

8. What emotions are you embarrassed to express to your loved ones?

9. What makes you feel defensive? What parts of yourself are you trying to protect?

10. What do you physically feel when you are scared or anxious?

11. What overwhelming emotions do you hide in social situations?

_____
_____
_____
_____
_____
_____

12. How are you feeling right now?

_____
_____
_____
_____
_____
_____

13. What is the most dominant emotion you feel now? How do you feel it in your body?

_____
_____
_____
_____
_____
_____

14. What triggered this emotion?

_____
_____
_____
_____
_____
_____

15. Do you have unresolved conflicts that affect your emotions? How do you deal with them?

16. What parts of yourself do you reject?

17. What parts of yourself do you judge harshly?

18. What emotions have you been carrying for so long, and do you need to release them?

19. What is the one emotion you wish you could share with others but are afraid of being judged?

_____
_____
_____
_____
_____
_____

20. Do you act angry, but underneath, you feel a different emotion? What is this emotion?

_____
_____
_____
_____
_____
_____

21. Do you feel that you have to hide certain emotions to be accepted?

_____
_____
_____
_____
_____
_____

22. Pick the emotions that resonate with you.

PICK THE EMOTIONS THAT RESONATE WITH YOU

- ☐ Fear
- ☐ Sadness
- ☐ Shame
- ☐ Anger
- ☐ Fear
- ☐ Guilt
- ☐ Emptiness
- ☐ Jealousy
- ☐ Frustration
- ☐ Loneliness
- ☐ Helplessness
- ☐ Inadequacy
- ☐ Anxiety
- ☐ Depression
- ☐ Failure
- ☐ Resentment

Past Experiences

Consider moments when you have felt rejected, judged, or misunderstood. This helps bring hidden wounds to the surface for exploration.

1. Think of a time when you felt rejected or unloved. How did you react to that experience, and how do you feel about it now?

   _____
   _____
   _____
   _____
   _____
   _____

2. Have you ever felt that you wanted to be someone else so people would love you?

   _____
   _____
   _____
   _____
   _____
   _____

3. Is there a moment you wish you could have said something, but you held back your words out of fear of being misunderstood or judged?

   _____
   _____
   _____
   _____
   _____
   _____

4. What past experience brings back feelings of anger, pain, or rejection?

_____
_____
_____
_____
_____
_____
_____

5. When was the last time you were hard on yourself? What made you feel that way?

_____
_____
_____
_____
_____
_____
_____

6. When was the last time you felt misunderstood? What prompted this emotion?

_____
_____
_____
_____
_____
_____
_____

7. When was the last time you were embarrassed of your emotions? Why did you feel that way?

_____
_____
_____
_____
_____
_____
_____

8. Have you ever manipulated others to hide your vulnerability or out of fear that people won't accept you?

_____
_____
_____
_____
_____
_____
_____

9. Why do you think that people won't love or accept your shadow self?

_____
_____
_____
_____
_____
_____
_____

10. Are you struggling with feeling unloved? What people or situations made you feel that way?

_____
_____
_____
_____
_____
_____
_____

11. Do you want to confront the people who rejected you? What would you tell them?

_____
_____
_____
_____
_____
_____
_____

12. What major life event made you feel judged, rejected, or misunderstood?

_____
_____
_____
_____
_____
_____

13. Are you purposely making people misunderstand you to hide aspects of your personality?

_____
_____
_____
_____
_____
_____

14. Has a loved one ever judged or rejected you? How did that make you feel? What do you wish you could tell them now?

_____
_____
_____
_____
_____
_____

15. When was the last time someone misunderstood you? How did it make you feel?

_____
_____
_____
_____
_____
_____

16. When was the last time you felt unloved? How did that make you feel?

17. What or who triggers feelings of rejection?

My Shadow Self-Profile

Imagine your shadow self as a real person and answer these questions.

1. What does your shadow self currently look like?

2. How does it act?

3. How does it react?

_____
_____
_____
_____
_____
_____

4. What triggers your shadow self?

_____
_____
_____
_____
_____
_____

5. What are the dominant traits of your shadow self?

_____
_____
_____
_____
_____
_____

6. Is your shadow self angry for being hidden? What does it want to say?

_____
_____
_____
_____
_____
_____

7. How does it react to criticism?

8. When was the last time you prevented your shadow self from expressing its emotions? How did that make it feel? What did it want to say?

9. Imagine hugging your shadow self and treating it with compassion. How does it feel now?

10. Draw what your shadow self looks like now.

11. Write a letter to your shadow self.

_____
_____
_____
_____
_____
_____
_____
_____
_____
_____
_____
_____
_____
_____
_____
_____
_____
_____

Your shadow self is a part of you. It represents your mistakes, anger, fears, and embarrassing moments. These aspects make you human. You can't avoid them all your life. Embrace your shadow self and accept it. It is hurt and broken, so treat it with love and compassion.

Section 2: ACCEPTANCE

Embrace Your Inner Wound

Your shadow self is shaped by emotional trauma, pain, and scars you carry with you. These are elements of your life you wish not to bring to the surface, and despite your efforts to stay away from them, you only risk feeling compromised. Accepting your wounds will enable you to feel whole.

Embracing your wounds will allow you to overcome them.[2]

This chapter addresses the approach to healing trauma by confronting emotional wounds. More importantly, it encourages you to take care of the parts that feel broken by providing stepping stones to identify and nurture the pain.

The Importance of Accepting Your Emotional Wounds

Acknowledging your emotional wounds is paramount to achieving integration and wholeness. The healing process requires you to embrace your emotional wounds and change your relationship with your pain, so what was an experience of suffering can ultimately be your greatest strength. You should not look at your past with regret. You must learn from it and get on with living your life. Emotional wounds are simply part of life. You cannot avoid emotional pain in your life. You must lose loved ones, miss out on hopes and dreams, and endure difficulties. Just as meaningful times are part of life, painful times are a noteworthy part of life. You must experience both sides of life to live it fully. When you try to live a life free from emotional pain, you will never feel whole. You will always feel like a piece of you is missing. Emotional wounds are part of your being. They are part of your lived experiences, and they are part of your life lessons. Accepting the brutality of life means you wholeheartedly accept all of yourself and all the life you have lived.

Most emotional wounds originate from early experiences, relationships, and social conditioning. For instance, if you loved someone and had a bad breakup, you may experience emotional pain each time you think of them. Abusive parents also leave emotional scars that time may not heal.

Many people struggle to move on from their past. They believe that healing requires forgetting the painful experiences or those who hurt them. Emotional healing is about forgiving yourself or others while carrying the lessons you have learned. Instead of holding on to the pain and letting it consume you, you transform it into compassion and wisdom. You allow your past to make you a better person, free of anger and regrets.

Benefits of Embracing Emotional Wounds
- Improve your physical health
- Increase resilience
- Boost your emotional intelligence
- Enhance mental health
- Reduce the risk of mental illness
- Increase productivity
- Healthy relationships
- Encouraging personal growth

Vulnerability and Self-Compassion

According to researcher Brené Brown, embracing your vulnerability can make you more resilient and help you lead an authentic life. She urges people to be kinder and more understanding towards themselves and practice self-compassion during tough times to overcome challenges.

Many people are afraid of showing their vulnerable side. However, Brown explains that vulnerability is a gift, not a weakness. Only courageous and confident individuals can share this part of themselves.

Being vulnerable involves sharing your deepest thoughts and feelings without fear of judgment or rejection. When you show people your most authentic self, you create a safe space for them to be vulnerable as well. This allows you to build strong relationships based on mutual trust.

Vulnerability allows you to unlock your full potential to become the person you have always wanted and achieve your goals. You will stop being afraid of failure, treat every mistake as a learning opportunity, and accept your strengths and weaknesses.

Brown also states that you can overcome negative emotions with self-compassion. When you are sad or have self-doubt, imagine someone you love is going through the same experience. Talk to yourself as if you are talking to them. Be kind, positive, and supportive.

Childhood Trauma

According to psychologist and philosopher Alice Miller, childhood trauma can have a huge impact on a person's life. The first three years of a child's life are crucial in their brain development. Traumatized children can become more stressed or violent.

If you've experienced trauma in your childhood, this is something you need to confront.⁹

Growing up with abusive parents who emotionally neglected and never validated or supported you can be traumatic. The emotional scars toxic parents leave can negatively impact every aspect of your life.

Don't let your past pain impact your future. Acknowledge your inner child's needs and give yourself the support and validation your parents didn't give you. Reclaim your emotional freedom and understand and accept your past to overcome its influence. When you heal your inner wounds, you give yourself the freedom to be happy and confident and build healthy relationships.

Healing from past wounds doesn't mean forgetting the pain. You are simply not letting it define you or ruin your present and future.

Prompts and Questions

The prompts and questions in this section will help you identify your emotional wounds, understand where they originated from, and begin the healing process with self-compassion.

Emotional Wounds From the Past

Identify the wounds you have carried all your life.

1. What are the deepest emotional wounds you carry?

2. How have these wounds shaped the way you view yourself and others?

3. Describe your childhood.

4. Were your parents warm and loving or cold and distant? How has their behavior affected you?

_____
_____
_____
_____
_____
_____
_____
_____

5. What do you feel when you think about your childhood?

_____
_____
_____
_____
_____
_____
_____
_____

6. How have your emotional wounds impacted your life and relationships?

_____
_____
_____
_____
_____
_____
_____
_____

7. Is there a past experience that makes you angry? Why?

_____
_____
_____
_____
_____
_____
_____

8. Do you wish you could get closure from a certain person? What do you want them to tell you?

_____
_____
_____
_____
_____
_____
_____
_____

9. Do you blame yourself for your emotional wounds? Why?

_____
_____
_____
_____
_____
_____
_____
_____

10. How does your inner child feel now?

_____
_____
_____
_____
_____
_____
_____
_____

11. What can you do to make it feel better?

_____
_____
_____
_____
_____
_____
_____
_____

12. What do you see when you look in the mirror?

_____
_____
_____
_____
_____
_____
_____
_____

13. Do you struggle with trusting others? Why?

14. How do your emotional wounds affect your mental and physical health?

15. What do you feel when you think about your emotional wounds?

16. If you could go back in time, what advice would you give your past self to protect them from these wounds?

_____
_____
_____
_____
_____
_____
_____
_____

Shame and Self-Criticism

Reflect on how shame might be affecting your healing.

1. In what areas of your life do you carry feelings of shame or self-blame?

_____
_____
_____
_____
_____
_____
_____
_____
_____

2. How can you begin to release these feelings and practice self-compassion?

_____
_____
_____
_____
_____
_____
_____
_____

3. Is there something in your life you blame yourself on? What is it?

_____
_____
_____
_____
_____
_____
_____
_____

4. How does shame affect your life?

_____
_____
_____
_____
_____
_____
_____

5. Do you blame yourself for every bad thing that happens to you? Why?

_____
_____
_____
_____
_____
_____
_____
_____
_____

6. What does your inner critic often tell you?

_____
_____
_____
_____
_____
_____
_____
_____

7. How do you silence this voice?

_____
_____
_____
_____
_____
_____
_____
_____

8. Do you judge yourself harshly? Why? What do you often say to yourself?

_____
_____
_____
_____
_____
_____
_____
_____

9. Do you use criticism to motivate yourself? Do you believe there are better ways to motivate yourself?

10. Does your shame or inner critic affect your healing? How?

11. When was the last time you criticized yourself? Write down the words you used.

12. How do shame and self-blame affect your life?

13. Write a letter to the part of yourself that feels shame.

14. Draw what shame feels like.

Forgiveness and Letting Go

Healing often requires forgiveness, both of others and yourself. Reflect on who or what you need to forgive to move forward.

1. Who do you need to forgive, including yourself, to truly heal?

_____
_____
_____
_____
_____
_____
_____
_____

2. How can you begin the process of letting go of past hurt?

_____
_____
_____
_____
_____
_____
_____
_____

3. What is the one mistake you can't forgive yourself for? How can you release it and move on?

_____
_____
_____
_____
_____
_____
_____
_____

4. Reflect on a time when someone forgave you. How did that make you feel?

_____
_____
_____
_____
_____
_____
_____
_____
_____

5. How do grudges affect your life? What can you do to move towards forgiveness?

_____
_____
_____
_____
_____
_____
_____
_____
_____

6. What can you do today to practice empathy and forgive someone who has hurt you?

_____
_____
_____
_____
_____
_____
_____
_____
_____

7. What can you let go of to be at peace?

_____
_____
_____
_____
_____
_____

8. What negative thoughts and beliefs are preventing you from forgiving yourself and others?

_____
_____
_____
_____
_____
_____
_____

9. Write a letter of forgiveness to someone who has hurt you.

_____
_____
_____
_____
_____
_____
_____
_____
_____
_____
_____
_____
_____
_____
_____

10. Write a letter of forgiveness to yourself.

_____
_____
_____
_____
_____
_____
_____
_____
_____
_____
_____
_____
_____
_____
_____
_____

The Impact of Past Trauma

Reflect on how past trauma has affected your life and answer these questions.

1. How has past trauma influenced your thoughts, behaviors, and relationships?

_____
_____
_____
_____
_____
_____
_____
_____

2. What steps can you take today to begin healing these old wounds?

_____
_____
_____
_____
_____
_____
_____
_____

3. How has your traumatic experience influenced your decisions?

_____
_____
_____
_____
_____
_____
_____
_____

4. How has your trauma affected your loved ones?

_____
_____
_____
_____
_____
_____
_____
_____

5. Imagine you have healed from your trauma. How does that make you feel?

_____
_____
_____
_____
_____
_____
_____
_____
_____

6. What does healing feel like?

_____
_____
_____
_____
_____
_____
_____
_____

7. How can you control your life and prevent your past from influencing your present?

_____
_____
_____
_____
_____
_____
_____
_____
_____

8. How would your life be different if you didn't experience that traumatic event?

_____
_____
_____
_____
_____
_____
_____
_____
_____

9. Write a letter to the person responsible for your trauma.

_____
_____
_____
_____
_____
_____
_____
_____
_____
_____
_____
_____
_____
_____
_____
_____
_____
_____
_____

10. Draw your past self and your future/desired self next to it.

Don't let your past wounds influence your present and future. Accept them, forgive yourself and others, and move on with your life.

Section 3: RELEASE

Cast Away Limiting Beliefs and Emotional Blockages

Have you ever caught yourself thinking you just aren't cut out for something—maybe because you believed you lacked the strength or smarts needed? Life tends to toss around those nagging ideas that keep you stuck. You end up doubting your talents, constantly questioning what you're capable of, and before you know it, you're trapped by these negative voices. Generally speaking, if you let that inner critic lead, you risk missing out on real rewards and end up with more regrets than wins.

Limiting beliefs hold you back from moving forward.'

In this chapter, we take a closer look at those limiting beliefs and their quiet yet steady hold on your everyday experiences. It shows you, in a pretty down-to-earth way, how to flip the script on those discouraging thoughts and, in most cases, clear out the emotional clutter that's been blocking your progress.

Limiting Beliefs

Limiting beliefs are the negative thoughts and assumptions you hold about yourself, others, or the world. In life, they drag you down, denying you access to your true potential. This pattern of thoughts usually develops at an early age from early experiences that shape us, the way we are brought up, failures that we have experienced, societal norms, or negative self-talk.

For example, a child with neglectful and emotionally detached parents may internalize the belief that they are unlovable. A girl growing up in a male-dominated society will think that she can't ever accomplish what she wants or go far in life.

Your decisions, your self-image, how you view things, and your interpretation of situations are all affected by limiting beliefs. They keep you from making leaps or seizing opportunities. Imagine your boss assigns you and other employees work and will promote whoever has the best idea. If you think that you aren't bright enough or will never be promoted, you will not put your best effort into the assignment, and this will obviously keep you from being promoted. The person who gets promoted may, in fact, not have the skill set or talent you possess, but they have believed in themselves and played the game.

You may also experience these thoughts about others. You may believe that all people are bad or that all marriages end in divorce. As a result, you will end up depriving yourself of genuine friendships or committed relationships.

Limiting beliefs can be a defense mechanism to protect you from pain. Let's say you had a negative experience in a few job interviews. You may stop going to new ones to protect yourself from disappointment or rejection.

These thoughts and perceptions lower your self-esteem and your motivation, keeping you stuck in patterns of fear or self-doubt.

Limiting beliefs aren't as powerful as you may think. While they can impact your life, they are nothing more than thought patterns that can be changed with reframing techniques.

Releasing limiting beliefs doesn't mean forgetting your past experiences. You are simply restructuring these thoughts to liberate yourself from their restricting hold.

Cognitive Reframing

Cognitive reframing is a technique that shifts your mindset and changes how you feel about a person, relationship, or situation. It focuses on your thought pattern to transform the negativity into positivity. Say you believe that you will never get promoted at work. You keep saying, "I am not good enough," or "I don't have the skills to advance in my career." You can use cognitive reframing and imagine yourself as a lawyer trying to find proof to contradict these thoughts. What evidence supports that you aren't good at your job? If you are a bad employee, why didn't they let you go? You will eventually realize that these thoughts have no basis.

Psychologist Dr. Aaron Beck developed the cognitive reframing technique in the 1960s to help patients suffering from depression think positively. He believed that your interpretation of a situation, not the situation itself, entices a reaction from you. For instance, a person may be upset when it rains because it prevents them from going out and seeing their friends. Others will see it as an opportunity to stay at home and play games or watch a movie with their family.

Your thoughts and actions don't define you. They represent your reaction to an event. You can control them if you change how you look and approach any situation.

Emotional Blockages

Emotional blockages keep you from feeling or expressing your emotions. Oftentimes, you don't understand how you feel or why you are experiencing a certain emotion. It is a defense mechanism that prevents you from accepting your emotions, thinking clearly, and reacting properly to a situation.

Emotional blockages usually occur when you avoid your emotions. When you ignore your feelings, they overpower you, leaving you angry, easily triggered, and confused. This can impact your relationships, mental health, career, social life, behavior, and cognitive skills. They can also hinder your personal growth, leaving you stagnant.

Releasing these blockages involves identifying their root causes.

Causes of Emotional Blockages
- Past experiences
- Societal conditioning
- Inner self-critic
- Negative thoughts
- Fear and anxiety
- Stress
- Traumatic experiences
- Serious diseases
- Surprising lifestyle changes
- Losing a job
- Breakup or divorce
- Death of a loved one

Psychologist and psychotherapist Dr. Peter Levine created a type of alternative therapy called "Somatic Experiencing" to help people suffering from trauma. He believed that trauma is stored in the body, causing mental, physical, and emotional issues.

Traumatic experiences can cause disconnection from one's body. Somatic experiencing involves using specific techniques that can bring awareness to your emotions, physical sensations, and internal experiences.

Prompts and Questions

The prompts and questions in this section will help you identify your limiting beliefs, explore their origins, and reframe them into empowering perspectives.

My Limiting Beliefs

Explore the beliefs that hold you back and change how you see yourself, your life, other people, experiences, etc., that are often buried beneath the surface.

1. What beliefs about yourself do you rarely share with others? When did you first start believing this about yourself?

2. How did past experiences or external influences shape this belief?

3. What beliefs are holding you back from achieving your goals or living the life you want?

4. Write down three limiting beliefs that affect your relationships.

_____
_____
_____
_____
_____
_____
_____
_____
_____

5. Write down three limiting beliefs that prevent you from advancing in your career.

_____
_____
_____
_____
_____
_____
_____
_____
_____

6. Write down three limiting beliefs that affect your social life.

_____
_____
_____
_____
_____
_____
_____
_____
_____

7. Write down three limiting beliefs you have about yourself.

_____
_____
_____
_____
_____
_____
_____
_____

8. Write down three limiting beliefs you have about your family.

_____
_____
_____
_____
_____
_____
_____
_____

9. Write down three limiting beliefs you have about your friends.

_____
_____
_____
_____
_____
_____
_____
_____

10. Write down three limiting beliefs you have about people in general.

_____
_____
_____
_____
_____
_____
_____
_____

11. Write down three limiting beliefs you have about life.

_____
_____
_____
_____
_____
_____
_____
_____

12. Reflect on your childhood; what limiting beliefs prevented you from achieving your goals? Where did they stem from?

_____
_____
_____
_____
_____
_____
_____
_____

13. When you think of limiting beliefs, do you hear your voice or your parent's or teacher's voice telling you that you aren't good enough?

_____
_____
_____
_____
_____
_____
_____
_____

14. Why do you give these beliefs so much power?

_____
_____
_____
_____
_____
_____
_____
_____

15. Are these your beliefs, or has someone influenced you, like society, friends, parents, etc.?

_____
_____
_____
_____
_____
_____
_____
_____

16. Are these beliefs helping you grow? How do they make your life better?

_____
_____
_____
_____
_____
_____
_____

17. Write down three opportunities you have missed or goals you couldn't achieve because of these beliefs.

_____
_____
_____
_____
_____
_____
_____

18. What can you do now to achieve these goals?

_____
_____
_____
_____
_____
_____
_____

19. What do your limiting beliefs protect you from?

20. Will you be happier if you let go of your limiting beliefs? Why?

21. How do your limiting beliefs affect your daily life?

22. What has your inner critic been telling you lately?

_____
_____
_____
_____
_____
_____
_____
_____

23. Do you believe your limiting beliefs have positive intentions? What are they?

_____
_____
_____
_____
_____
_____
_____
_____

24. When you think of your story, what words do you use to describe yourself and your life?

_____
_____
_____
_____
_____
_____
_____
_____

25. Write a farewell letter to one of your most powerful limiting beliefs. Thank it for its internet and express how it has influenced your life. Explain that it's time now to move on from it to another belief that will help you on the next part of your journey.

_____
_____
_____
_____
_____
_____
_____
_____
_____
_____
_____
_____
_____
_____
_____
_____
_____

Reframing Limiting Beliefs

Challenge and reframe your limiting beliefs into more positive and empowering thoughts.

1. Write one limiting belief.

_____
_____
_____
_____
_____
_____
_____
_____

2. Acknowledge that it is a limiting belief, not a fact.

_____
_____
_____
_____
_____
_____
_____
_____

3. How does this limiting belief make you feel?

_____
_____
_____
_____
_____
_____
_____
_____

4. How does it impact your life?

_____
_____
_____
_____
_____
_____
_____
_____

5. Where does this belief stem from?

_____
_____
_____
_____
_____
_____
_____
_____

6. Is this belief true? Write down why you think it is or isn't true.

_____
_____
_____
_____
_____
_____
_____
_____

7. If you believe it is true, you can question it. Write down three or four questions and their answers to prove whether it is based on facts or negative thoughts.

_____
_____
_____
_____
_____
_____
_____
_____

8. Imagine letting go of this belief. How does that make you feel?

_____
_____
_____
_____
_____
_____
_____
_____

9. How will you challenge future limiting beliefs?

_____
_____
_____
_____
_____
_____
_____
_____

10. How does it feel to replace limiting beliefs with positive thoughts?

_____
_____
_____
_____
_____
_____
_____
_____

11. What small steps can you take to move away from these beliefs?

___

12. Mention some of your most empowering beliefs.

___

13. Imagine a life without your limiting beliefs. What does this version of you believe in and feel?

___

14. How can these beliefs serve you now?

15. Describe a perfect day without these limiting beliefs.

16. What would you be doing right now if your limiting beliefs didn't exist?

17. Think of some of your limiting beliefs. Rephrase them to become more positive and empowering.

18. What would you do now if these positive and empowering statements were true?

19. How can you use these positive beliefs instead of the old ones?

20. How can you learn from your mistakes instead of allowing them to reinforce your limiting beliefs?

_____
_____
_____
_____
_____
_____
_____
_____

21. What makes you get up in the morning?

_____
_____
_____
_____
_____
_____
_____
_____

22. What if your limiting beliefs were true? What is the worst that could happen?

_____
_____
_____
_____
_____
_____
_____
_____

23. How can you save yourself from this worst-case scenario? Write down in detail what you will do if something bad happens. (This will show you that even if one limiting belief is true, you can always salvage the situation, removing the power of this belief.)

_____
_____
_____
_____
_____
_____
_____

Reframing With Affirmations of Empowerment

Affirmations are short and positive statements that can change your thought pattern, helping you adopt a more confident mindset. You should repeat them every day multiple times to overpower your negative beliefs.

1. Write down five affirmations that you will repeat each time you experience this limiting belief.

_____
_____
_____
_____
_____
_____
_____

2. How can you remind yourself daily of your worth and potential?

_____
_____
_____
_____
_____
_____
_____

3. What positive words do you use to describe yourself and your achievements?

_____
_____
_____
_____
_____
_____
_____
_____

4. Write three things about your life for which you are grateful.

_____
_____
_____
_____
_____
_____
_____
_____

5. What makes you the most proud of yourself?

_____
_____
_____
_____
_____
_____
_____
_____

Affirmations
- I am letting go of my limiting beliefs
- I can overcome challenges
- I question my negative beliefs
- I am smart and successful
- My mistakes don't define me
- I am in control of my thoughts
- I deserve to be happy
- I have what it takes to achieve my goals
- I seize every opportunity that comes my way
- I make a positive impact on people's lives
- I have people in my life who love me and want the best for me
- I am grateful for my life
- I am enough
- I love myself
- I trust my skills and abilities
- I am where I am supposed to be

Confronting Emotional Blockages

Reflect on unresolved emotions that might be holding them back.

1. What emotions have you been suppressing or avoiding?

_____
_____
_____
_____
_____
_____
_____
_____

2. How can you create a safe space to process and release these feelings?

_____
_____
_____
_____
_____
_____
_____
_____
_____

3. Are you distracting yourself from your true feelings? How?

_____
_____
_____
_____
_____
_____
_____
_____
_____

4. Do you struggle with communicating your feelings? If yes, why?

_____
_____
_____
_____
_____
_____
_____
_____
_____

5. What emotions do you struggle with expressing the most? Why?

_____
_____
_____
_____
_____
_____
_____
_____

6. How different would your life be if you could express your emotions?

_____
_____
_____
_____
_____
_____
_____

7. How do you feel right now?

_____
_____
_____
_____
_____
_____
_____
_____
_____

8. When was the last time you felt happy and safe?

_____
_____
_____
_____
_____
_____

9. When was the last time you cried? Did you cry in front of others or alone?

_____
_____
_____
_____
_____
_____

10. Write a "letter of release" to yourself or someone connected to the blocked emotion, expressing everything you have been holding in. You can then destroy the letter as a symbolic act of letting go.

_____
_____
_____
_____
_____
_____
_____
_____
_____
_____
_____
_____
_____

Breaking Free from Fear

Address the fears that prevent you from changing and growing.

1. What fears keep you stuck in old patterns?

   _____
   _____
   _____
   _____
   _____

2. What would it feel like to move past these fears?

   _____
   _____
   _____
   _____
   _____

3. How are your fears preventing you from changing and growing?

   _____
   _____
   _____
   _____
   _____

4. What would your life be like if your fears didn't control you?

   _____
   _____
   _____
   _____
   _____

5. Where do these fears stem from?

   _____
   _____
   _____
   _____
   _____

6. When was the last time your fear prevented you from achieving a goal?

_____
_____
_____
_____
_____

7. What is your biggest fear?

_____
_____
_____
_____
_____

8. Is this fear real or the result of negative thoughts, your upbringing, or society's influence?

_____
_____
_____
_____
_____

9. How can you overcome this fear?

_____
_____
_____
_____
_____

10. Describe how it would feel to be free from your fears.

_____
_____
_____
_____
_____

11. What do your fears tell you each time you try to change or get out of your comfort zone?

_____
_____
_____
_____
_____

Releasing Through the Body

Emotional blockages are connected to physical tension. Your suppressed emotions can give you headaches and make you tired.

1. Where in your body do you feel tension or discomfort when you think about your blockages?

_____
_____
_____
_____
_____

2. What can you do to release this energy?

_____
_____
_____
_____
_____

3. How do you feel when you release this energy?

_____
_____
_____
_____
_____

4. What emotions manifest physically?

_____
_____
_____
_____
_____

5. Does each emotion have a different sensation?

_____
_____
_____
_____
_____

6. Have you tried talking about your emotions when they manifested physically? How did that make you feel?

_____
_____
_____
_____
_____

Limiting beliefs aren't facts. They are negative thoughts manipulating you to make you question your abilities. Reframe the negativity with positivity and focus on what you can do instead of what you can't do.

Section 4: INTEGRATION

Merge with All Parts of You

Every part of you deserves to be loved. You need to embrace your darkness and weakness to appreciate your light and strength. Personal growth requires self-acceptance and respecting all different aspects of your personality.

Embrace your darkness and weaknesses to find your strength for self-love.[5]

This chapter explains the concept of integration and individualism. You will also find various prompts to help you find balance between your light and shadow, embrace your imperfection, and find self-acceptance.

Self-Integration

Self-integration is creating a balanced relationship with all aspects of your personality. It involves acknowledging your neglected parts and integrating your positive and negative sides.

You can't live a fulfilling life if you hide one part of yourself. Integrating your light and darkness is essential to make you whole. Self-integration is a crucial part of shadow work. It harmonizes your behavior, values, actions, thoughts, and emotions to make you feel complete. This allows you to thrive in every aspect of your life without suppressing or denying your authentic self. When you are at peace with every aspect of yourself, everything in your life works smoothly.

Self-integration leads to self-love, self-awareness, self-acceptance, clarity, and a deeper understanding of the self. It involves observing your different experiences, emotions, and thoughts without judgment. You acknowledge and engage with every aspect of your personality, even the frustrating ones.

When you are self-integrated, all aspects of your personality are unified. You love every part of you, allowing you to thrive and live happily.

Self-integration is different from perfection. It is about finding peace and accepting all parts of yourself without rejecting your mistakes or trying to be perfect.

Disintegration, on the other hand, causes imbalance since every part of you is competing with the other instead of working together.

Principles of Self-Integration

- Taking responsibility for your decisions, actions, and mistakes.
- Living in alignment with your needs and values.
- Embracing your authentic self no matter how challenging life gets.
- Understanding that every aspect of your personality makes you whole, even the parts that contradict each other. You should accept and listen to each one of them.

Benefits of Integration
- Mental stability
- Peace of mind
- Lack of mental health issues like depression and anxiety
- Decision-making skills
- Maintaining healthy relationships
- Clarity
- Having purpose
- High self-esteem
- Consistent behavior
- Ability to resist external influences
- Reduced stress and exhaustion
- High productivity
- Spiritual connection

Carl Jung's Concept of Individuation

According to Carl Jung, individuation is when a person becomes an individual, separate from the whole. It involves recognizing your unique characteristics and becoming your own authentic self. This allows you to accept your consciousness and the unconscious. The purpose of individuation is to develop your personality and let go of the false persona you use in public.

Jung created this concept from personal experience. He had a midlife crisis that drove him to confront different aspects of his personality; Jung spent years trying to understand himself and become a better person.

Individuation takes you on a journey to understand yourself better. It allows you to become the most integrated version of your unique self and integrates the unconscious parts of the self into conscious awareness. It reveals who you are underneath the mask you wear to hide your negative side. You answer the question of who you would be if you made peace with your deepest secrets, darkest desires, and biggest mistakes.

The individuation process happens naturally. You don't choose to walk this path; life pushes you to it to learn, change, and grow.

Dr. Kristin Neff's Work on Self-Compassion

According to Dr. Kristin Neff, self-compassion is showing kindness and compassion to oneself. You treat yourself with love and understanding instead of listening to your inner critic every time you make a mistake or fail. You become your biggest cheerleader and support yourself during hard times instead of being judgemental or feeling defeated in the face of adversity.

Self-compassion can be a coping mechanism in tough situations and helps you become more resilient. It improves your physical and mental health and encourages you to make changes, grow, achieve your goals, and do everything in your power to be happy.

Prompts and Questions

The prompts and questions in this section help you explore the integration of your light and dark sides. They invite you to reflect on your imperfections, acknowledge your past wounds, and integrate all aspects of your personality to start healing.

Balancing Light and Shadow

Reflect on the parts of yourself you have rejected or suppressed to achieve a more balanced understanding of your identity.

1. What aspects of your personality are you struggling to acknowledge?

2. How can accepting these parts make you whole?

3. Do you have a dark side that scares you?

_____
_____
_____
_____

4. What parts of yourself have you rejected, and how can you start accepting them?

_____
_____
_____
_____

5. What parts of yourself are you proud of, and which ones are you trying to avoid?

_____
_____
_____
_____

6. Do you feel that your light and dark side are competing or getting along?

_____
_____
_____
_____

7. Imagine your dark and light sides as people. What do they look like?

_____
_____
_____
_____

8. What are their most dominant characteristics?

_____
_____
_____
_____

9. What can you do to integrate them?

_____
_____
_____
_____

10. Describe your light side in five words.

_____
_____
_____
_____

11. Describe your shadow side in five words.

_____
_____
_____
_____

12. Imagine your light side writing a letter to your shadow side to make it feel loved and accepted. What would it say?

_____
_____
_____
_____
_____
_____
_____
_____

13. Create two drawings that represent contrasting aspects of yourself. One can represent your "light" self (positive traits, strengths, or joyful moments), and the other can represent your "shadow" self (hidden fears, doubts, or perceived weaknesses).

Embracing Imperfection

Integration involves accepting your imperfections. You need to self-reflect on your flaws and love every part of you.

1. How has striving for perfection hindered your personal growth?

___

2. How might embracing your imperfections support your journey toward self-acceptance?

___

3. What high standards do you constantly hold yourself to?

___

4. Which of these high standards do you find unrealistic?

___

5. Is your perfection holding you back?

___

6. Why are you afraid of embracing your mistakes and flaws?

_____
_____
_____
_____
_____

7. How do you feel when you think of embracing your imperfections?

_____
_____
_____
_____
_____

8. What would your life be like if you accepted your imperfections?

_____
_____
_____
_____
_____

9. How do you feel when you make a mistake or when something isn't perfect?

_____
_____
_____
_____
_____

10. What would you tell a friend struggling with embracing imperfections?

_____
_____
_____
_____
_____

11. How does your fear of imperfections hold you back in life?

_____
_____
_____
_____

12. Do you struggle with accepting your imperfections out of fear of judgment?

_____
_____
_____
_____

13. How can you forgive your imperfections?

_____
_____
_____
_____

14. What is your fear of imperfection protecting you from?

_____
_____
_____
_____

15. What do you think will happen if you make a mistake?

_____
_____
_____
_____

16. How would your life change if people saw your imperfections?

_____
_____
_____
_____

17. What parts of your life would improve if you embraced your imperfections?

_____
_____
_____
_____

18. Why do your imperfections scare you?

_____
_____
_____
_____

19. Does your family, society, or environment influence your fear of imperfection? In what way?

_____
_____
_____
_____

20. What would happen if you, your work, or your life were imperfect?

_____
_____
_____
_____

Gratitude for Imperfection Journaling

Every day, write down moments where you embrace imperfection, like leaving your hair messy, making a mistake, or not meeting your usual standards, and choose to practice self-compassion instead.

_____
_____
_____
_____
_____
_____
_____
_____
_____
_____
_____
_____
_____
_____
_____

Compassionate Self-Acceptance

Self-compassion is a way to foster integration. Always be kind and compassionate to yourself.

1. How do you treat yourself when you make a mistake?

_____
_____
_____
_____

2. What would it look like if you treated yourself with the same compassion you offered others?

_____
_____
_____
_____
_____

3. What do you like about yourself?

_____
_____
_____
_____
_____

4. What don't you like about yourself? Is it worth changing?

_____
_____
_____
_____
_____

5. If you can change it, how can you improve yourself?

_____
_____
_____
_____
_____

6. If you can't change it, how can you make peace with it?

_____
_____
_____
_____
_____

7. How do you respect yourself?

_____
_____
_____
_____

8. Do you hold yourself to unrealistic high standards?

_____
_____
_____
_____
_____

9. How do you practice self-care every day?

_____
_____
_____
_____
_____

10. Write five things you love about yourself.

_____
_____
_____
_____
_____

11. When was the last time you practiced self-compassion? What did you tell yourself?

_____
_____
_____
_____
_____

12. Imagine you failed at something; what would you tell yourself to feel better?

_____
_____
_____
_____
_____

13. How do you silence your inner self-critic?

_____
_____
_____
_____
_____

14. How can you support yourself better?

_____
_____
_____
_____
_____

15. Write down ten things you are grateful for.

_____
_____
_____
_____
_____

16. When was the last time you felt proud of yourself? Write how you felt.

_____
_____
_____
_____
_____

17. Write a letter to your past self expressing compassion for their inner struggles.

18. Think of the last time you struggled with self-acceptance and write a compassionate letter to yourself.

Merge all parts of you and accept every aspect of your personality. Integrate your light and dark sides and embrace your flaws. Practice self-compassion and be kind to yourself.

Section 5: AUTHENTICITY

Step Into Your True Self

Who are you, really? This is a simple question, isn't it? Well, think again. Most people think they know their true selves. However, when you have been suppressing a part of you for so long, you may not be aware of various aspects of your personality. You may be oblivious to what you are capable of or your true potential.

When you are authentic, you can live a care-free and fulfilling life."

Now that you have integrated your light and shadow self, you are ready to live an authentic life. You can align your values with your lifestyle, overcome your fears, and ignore societal expectations to live a fulfilling life.

This chapter explains the concept of authenticity and provides prompts to help you live your life according to your core beliefs, embrace vulnerability, overcome expectations, and honor your passions.

What Is Authenticity?

Authenticity is self-determination and self-awareness that aligns your actions, decisions, and lifestyle with your core values, beliefs, and inner truths. Living an authentic life can have a huge impact on your mental, emotional, and physical health. It is a priority for your well-being – like food, water, and sleep. You drink water because you listen to your body's needs. Similarly, being authentic fulfills your emotional needs.

An authentic person lives in the moment, is fully aware of their internal experience, and understands their emotions, thoughts, and behavior. They constantly reflect on whether their actions and reactions align with their psychological needs and values. Authentic people understand the many aspects of their personality and make sure that their lifestyle aligns with each one of them.

Multiple philosophers had different interpretations of the word "Authenticity." German philosopher Martin Heidegger said that authenticity is accepting who you truly are and living up to your full potential. French existentialist Jean-Paul Sartre said that people are free to be whoever they want and interpret their experiences however they like. Danish philosopher Søren Kierkegaard described it as breaking free from societal and cultural restraint.

According to Brené Brown, authenticity is a choice that you have to make every day. Either wear a mask and be someone you are not, or be yourself and let the world see the real you. She stated that authentic individuals accept themselves for who they are. They are aware of their imperfections and share them with no shame or judgment.

Authentic people dare to be vulnerable and imperfect. They aren't ashamed of their deep thoughts and emotions or afraid of letting others see their flaws or mistakes. They know that they are worthy of love and acceptance for who they truly are, not for who they pretend to be.

Who is the real you? To answer this question, you must reflect on your most honest and aligned self. Imagine your life when you are unapologetically yourself. Your words, clothes, actions, etc., reflect your authentic self, not what others expect from you. You don't think of other people's opinions when picking an outfit or making a decision.

However, being authentic is different from being perfect. You don't try to be someone who doesn't make mistakes or always says and does the right thing. You simply live your life in a way that feels true and meaningful to you, which usually means taking risks and making mistakes.

Authentic people know they are flawed and don't pretend to be perfect versions of themselves.

According to psychologist Dr. Carl Rogers, a person can't change or move away from their true self until they accept who they are. He introduced the concept of congruence, which is the harmony between one's inner experience and outward expression. It's when your emotions, thoughts, and physical sensations align with each other.

Congruence is being authentic and transparent around people. You present yourself honestly and openly without lying or pretending to be someone you aren't. You share your true feelings and thoughts without fear of judgment to create genuine and trusting relationships with others. When you are real and honest, people will feel comfortable around you and open up to you.

Authenticity is like a smile. It invites everyone in the room to reciprocate the same behavior.

Prompts and Questions

The prompts and questions in this section help you identify your true values, passions, and purpose while addressing fears or obstacles you may face while trying to be authentic.

Living in Alignment with Core Values

Identify the values and principles that are most important to you.

1. What values are most central to who you are?

_____
_____
_____
_____
_____

2. How can you ensure your actions and choices reflect these values?

___

3. What is the first thing that comes to mind when you hear the word "Values"?

___

4. Mention the last time you were aligned with your values.

___

5. Write down your top five values and mention why they are important to you. Reflect on how these are currently being honored (or neglected) in different areas of your life.

___

6. How do these values align with your choices and lifestyle?

___

7. Which areas of your life don't align with your values?

_____
_____
_____
_____
_____

8. What makes you feel fulfilled?

_____
_____
_____
_____
_____

9. What issues make you angry?

_____
_____
_____
_____
_____

10. Are you living in alignment with your values today?

_____
_____
_____
_____
_____

11. What happens when you neglect your values?

_____
_____
_____
_____
_____

12. What can you do to be in alignment with your values?

_____
_____
_____
_____

13. What three changes can you make to live according to your values?

_____
_____
_____
_____

14. If you could change one thing about the world, what would it be? Why?

_____
_____
_____
_____

15. Mention someone you admire for their values and why.

_____
_____
_____
_____

16. Mention a book that inspired you to question your values.

_____
_____
_____
_____

17. If you could change one thing about yourself, what would it be and why?

_____
_____
_____
_____

18. What did you learn from your most painful experiences?

_____
_____
_____
_____
_____
_____

Embracing Vulnerability and Courage

Explore the role of vulnerability in living authentically and how you can find the courage to express your true self.

1. In what areas of your life are you holding back your true self?

_____
_____
_____
_____
_____

2. What small steps can you take to show up more authentically?

_____
_____
_____
_____
_____

3. Do you struggle with being vulnerable around others? Why?

_____
_____
_____
_____
_____

4. Are there people you are comfortable being your truest self around? Why?

_____
_____
_____
_____

5. Why aren't you comfortable around others?

_____
_____
_____
_____

6. How do you find the courage to be your authentic self?

_____
_____
_____
_____

7. What steps do you take every day to live an authentic life?

_____
_____
_____
_____

8. What or who holds you back from expressing your true self?

_____
_____
_____
_____

9. What does being authentic mean to you?

_____
_____
_____
_____

10. When was the last time you struggled to express your true self? Why did you feel this way?

_____
_____
_____
_____

11. When was the last time you were in alignment with your authentic self?

_____
_____
_____
_____

12. Who were you with? How did you feel?

_____
_____
_____
_____

13. What gave you the courage to be open and honest?

_____
_____
_____
_____

Overcoming External Expectations

Reflect on societal, familial, or peer pressures that might be holding you back from authenticity.

1. What expectations have you internalized from others?

   _____
   _____
   _____
   _____
   _____

2. How can you begin to prioritize your own truth over external validation?

   _____
   _____
   _____
   _____
   _____

3. Did your parents set unrealistic high standards for you? How do you deal with them?

   _____
   _____
   _____
   _____
   _____

4. Do you struggle with being your true self due to peer pressure or society's expectations?

   _____
   _____
   _____
   _____
   _____

5. Do you dress or speak differently around certain people? Why?

_____
_____
_____
_____

6. When was the last time you didn't express your opinion out of fear of being judged? What went through your mind during that moment?

_____
_____
_____
_____

7. What do you think would happen if people saw the real you?

_____
_____
_____
_____

8. Why do you care about other people's opinions?

_____
_____
_____
_____

9. Who are you when no one is around? Which person do you like better: the private one or the public one?

_____
_____
_____
_____

10. Write a letter to your future self, imagining what your most authentic life looks like and what steps you will take to get there.

_____
_____
_____
_____
_____
_____
_____
_____
_____
_____
_____
_____
_____
_____
_____
_____
_____

Discovering and Honoring Passions

Explore what truly excites you and how you can incorporate these passions into your life.

1. What activities or experiences make you feel alive and connected to yourself?

_____
_____
_____
_____

2. How can you incorporate these into your daily or weekly routine?

_____
_____
_____
_____

3. Do you have a hobby that you keep private out of fear of being judged? What makes you feel this way?

_____
_____
_____
_____

4. Mention three hobbies that give you joy.

_____
_____
_____
_____

5. If money wasn't an issue, what would you be doing now?

_____
_____
_____
_____

6. If someone hired a private detective to follow you, what would they say you spend your time doing?

_____
_____
_____
_____

7. What is your biggest passion?

_____
_____
_____
_____

8. What makes you feel your best self?

_____
_____
_____
_____

9. What is your favorite place in the world?

_____
_____
_____
_____

10. What activity makes you lose track of time?

_____
_____
_____
_____

11. Describe your perfect day.

_____
_____
_____
_____

12. Describe something or someone that makes you feel like a child again.

_____
_____
_____
_____
_____

13. Think of the last time you laughed from your heart; what were you doing?

_____
_____
_____
_____
_____

14. If you could live anywhere in the world, where would that be? Why would you want to live there?

_____
_____
_____
_____
_____

15. What activities did you enjoy doing as a child?

_____
_____
_____
_____
_____

16. What was your dream career as a child?

_____
_____
_____
_____

17. What would you do if you couldn't fail?

_____
_____
_____
_____
_____

18. What do you regret not trying?

_____
_____
_____
_____
_____

19. Picture your perfect life. Who are you with, and what are you doing?

_____
_____
_____
_____
_____

20. What goals would you accomplish now if you had the time and resources?

_____
_____
_____
_____
_____

21. Create a vision board to visually represent your authentic life, including your dreams, values, and goals.

Your true self is your best self. Love and nourish it. Have the courage to share it with the world. If someone doesn't like you, it's their problem, not yours. Don't let people's opinions or judgments influence who you want to be.

Conclusion

Embracing your shadow self can be challenging. Many people struggle to make peace with their past mistakes and trauma. Instead of confronting their weaknesses and darkness, they choose to hide and ignore them. They are afraid of being judged or misunderstood.

You can't live your life hiding from your true self. Everyone has parts of themselves that they are embarrassed by and wish they could keep private. However, confident and mentally strong individuals embrace their shadow selves. They find no shame in expressing their emotions and showing their vulnerable side.

The book took you on a journey to explore yourself and meet your true self. It explained the concept of the shadow self and the significance of acknowledging and confronting the hidden aspects of your personality. You should be brave enough to face your emotions, experiences, and beliefs.

Confronting the shadow self may feel like a punishment. However, it will help set you free from your past traumatic experience.

Your inner wounds can scar and traumatize your shadow self. You can't avoid pain for the rest of your life, but you can nurture your broken parts and heal. The book explained the importance of accepting, embracing, and healing your emotional wounds.

You can recover from your trauma and move on from unhealthy relationships and bad experiences. Healing doesn't mean that you have forgotten your past. You can heal while still holding onto the lessons from your past mistakes. You learned to use the prompts in the book to transform your pain into power.

Many people have limiting beliefs that make them feel they aren't good, strong, or smart enough. These prevent them from recognizing their true potential and living a fulfilling life. The book explained that these negative thoughts can hinder your growth. Using the journal prompts, you were able to reframe your limiting beliefs.

You can't heal your shadow self or grow without self-acceptance. You learned how you can accept your dark side and light side, strengths and weaknesses. You can embrace every part of yourself without judgment.

Creating a balanced relationship between both sides of your personality can help you become whole and achieve peace.

The last part of the book answered the question, "Who is the real you?" You learned how to accept your authentic self and live with courage and vulnerability.

You finished the book, but your self-exploration journey isn't over. Keep learning about yourself, healing, and growing. Continue embracing and loving your shadow self, and you will notice a change in your mental and emotional health.

If you enjoyed this book, I'd greatly appreciate a review on Amazon because it helps me to create more books that people want. It would mean a lot to hear from you.

To leave a review:
1. Open your camera app.
2. Point your mobile device at the QR code.
3. The review page will appear in your web browser.

Thanks for your support!

Here's another book by Mari Silva that you might like

Your Free Gift
(only available for a limited time)

Thanks for getting this book! If you want to learn more about various spirituality topics, then join Mari Silva's community and get a free guided meditation MP3 for awakening your third eye. This guided meditation mp3 is designed to open and strengthen ones third eye so you can experience a higher state of consciousness. Simply visit the link below the image to get started.

https://spiritualityspot.com/meditation
Or, Scan the QR code!

References

10 Journal Prompts for Breaking or Overcoming Limiting Beliefs. (2023, April 4). HolisticNiss. https://www.holisticniss.com/blog/overcome-limiting-beliefs

15 Journal Prompts For Self-Compassion. (2021, May 21). Dreaming by Dusk. https://www.dreamingbydusk.com/blog/journal-prompts-for-self-compassion

Alexa. (2022, December 12). 14 Journal Prompts for Limiting Beliefs - Ambitiously Alexa. Ambitiouslyalexa.com. https://ambitiouslyalexa.com/journal-prompts-for-limiting-beliefs/

Alice Miller: The Childhood Trauma: The Zero 5.0laf - The Official Website of Andrew Vachss. (2024). Vachss.com. https://www.vachss.com/guest_dispatches/alice_miller2.html

Bachert, A. (2024, May 9). Cognitive Reframing: 3 Steps to Change Your Perspective. Rula. https://www.rula.com/blog/cognitive-reframing/

Baldwin, M. (2022, March 30). What the New Science of Authenticity Says about Discovering Your True Self. The Conversation. https://theconversation.com/what-the-new-science-of-authenticity-says-about-discovering-your-true-self-175314

Biesalski, C. (n.d.). Shadow Work: What It is and How to Do It > The Essential Guide! CONNI BIESALSKI. https://www.conni.me/blog/shadow-work

Blanchfield, T. (2024, February 7). What to Know About Somatic Experiencing Therapy. Verywell Mind. https://www.verywellmind.com/what-is-somatic-experiencing-5204186

Brem, P. (2023, May 2). Embracing Vulnerability and Self-Compassion for Resilience and Growth. Linkedin.com.

https://www.linkedin.com/pulse/embracing-vulnerability-self-compassion-resilience-growth-brem-msc/

Brené Brown - How to Be Yourself. (2014, July 21). Oprah.com. https://www.oprah.com/inspiration/brene-brown-how-to-be-yourself_1

Clover, M. (2023, June 15). 25 Shadow Work Journal Prompts To Discover Your True Self. Molly Clover. https://mollyclover.com/25-shadow-work-journal-prompts-to-discover-your-true-self/

Coelho, S. (2020, May 27). Journaling For Emotional Health: 12 Writing Prompts. Psych Central. https://psychcentral.com/blog/journal-prompts-to-heal-emotions#healing-heartbreak

Congruence and Genuineness in Psychotherapy. (2024, February). Socialworktestprep.com; Social Work Test Prep. https://socialworktestprep.com/blog/2024/february/01/congruence-and-genuineness-in-psychotherapy/?srsltid=AfmBOorK1VRGYuUYjtGJfMTGAV7ZeMYFgMzJa5AtHNZILukd4jaKclqo

Courtney Harris Coaching. (2020, June 23). 12 Affirmations to Use When You Are Facing Self-Doubt -. Courtney Harris Coaching. https://courtneyharriscoaching.com/12-affirming-beliefs-for-getting-out-of-competition-and-into-connection/

Cy, S. (2017, December 24). 22 Thought-Provoking Journal Prompts to Clarify Your Worldview, Increase Your Motivation, and Discover Your Unique Purpose. Medium; The Writing Cooperative. https://writingcooperative.com/22-thought-provoking-journal-prompts-to-clarify-your-worldview-increase-your-motivation-and-aa879f9568c8

Dickeson, L. (2020, June 11). Congruence and Incongruence - How to Believe You're Good Enough | Ranch Hands Rescue. Ranch Hands Rescue. https://ranchhandsrescue.org/congruence/

Dubin, K. (2024, November 20). Healing from Emotional Neglect: Understanding Inner Child Wounds and Reclaiming Emotional Freedom - SWEET INSTITUTE - Continuing Education for Mental Health Professionals. SWEET INSTITUTE - Continuing Education for Mental Health Professionals - the One Stop Shop for Mental Health Clinicians and Agencies. https://sweetinstitute.com/healing-from-emotional-neglect-understanding-inner-child-wounds-and-reclaiming-emotional-freedom/

Fagan, D. (n.d.). Journal prompts & ideas for emotional release. My TMS Journey. https://mytmsjourney.com/resources/journal-prompts-ideas-for-emotional-release/

Friedrich, S. (2023, November 23). Self-Compassion Journaling Prompts: 101 Ways To Be Kinder. Writing by Saskia. https://writingbysaskia.com/self-compassion-journaling-prompts/

Gemma. (2022, May 2). Journaling for Well-being: Your Authentic Self. Gemma Brown Coaching. https://www.gemmabrowncoaching.co.uk/post/journaling-for-well-being-your-authentic-self

Glass, L. J. (2024, August 15). Emotional Blockage: How To Find Release. PIVOT. https://www.lovetopivot.com/what-causes-emotional-blockage/

Green, R. (2023, April 27). How to Live with Authenticity and Be Your Truest Self. Verywell Mind. https://www.verywellmind.com/live-with-authenticity-7483232

Griffiths, N. (2021, January 11). 31 Days of Shadow Work Journal Prompts For Healing and Growth. Seeking Serotonin. https://seekingserotonin.com/shadow-work-journal-prompts/

Hagen, P. (2024, August 21). 47 Journal Prompts for Emotional Awareness – Hagen Growth. Hagen Growth. https://hagengrowth.com/journal-prompts-for-emotional-awareness/

Hammer, B. (2015). Healing Our Emotional Pain and Relationship Pain. Journal of Psychology & Clinical Psychiatry, 2(5). https://doi.org/10.15406/jpcpy.2015.02.00091

Hannah, D. (2024, August 5). Self-Integration: The Important Pathway To Inner Wholeness. Symbosity. https://symbosity.com/how-to-achieve-self-integration/#penci-What_does_it_mean_to_be_self-integrated

Jeffrey, S. (2019, January 11). A Closer Look at Carl Jung's Individuation Process: A Map for Psychic Wholeness. Scott Jeffrey. https://scottjeffrey.com/individuation-process/

Jordan. (n.d.). Understand Your Values and Beliefs with Helpful Journal Prompts. Spirited Earthling. https://www.spiritedearthling.com/mindfulness-and-meditation/understand-your-values-and-beliefs-with-helpful-journal-prompts

Kristen Webb Wright. (2023, October 13). Beyond Perfectionism: 30 Journal Prompts for Self-Compassion. Day One | Your Journal for Life. https://dayoneapp.com/blog/perfectionism/

KW Marketing Team. (2021, January 10). 10 Positive Affirmations to Help You Crush Your Limiting Beliefs. KW Outfront Magazine. https://outfront.kw.com/training/10-affirmations-to-help-you-crush-your-limiting-beliefs/

LaVine, R. (2023, March 28). 100+ Deep Shadow Work Prompts To Accept Yourself And Move Forward. Science of People. https://www.scienceofpeople.com/shadow-work-prompts/

Luoma, J. (2017, October 5). Self-Enquiry into Self-criticism, Self-blame, and Shame. ACT with Compassion.

https://www.actwithcompassion.com/self_enquiry_into_self_criticism_self_blame_and_shame

M, S. (2023, December 20). 50 Self-Compassion Journal Prompts for Inner Growth. Little Crystals | Happiness, Harmony, and Balance. https://littlecrystals.com/blogs/news/self-compassion-journal-prompts

Martin, S. (2019, July 19). Reflective Questions to Help You Quiet Your Inner Perfectionist. Psych Central. https://psychcentral.com/blog/imperfect/2019/07/reflective-questions-to-help-you-quiet-your-inner-perfectionist#Shift-your-negative-thinking

Matheka, W. (2023, March 18). Journal Prompts for Inner Child Healing. Wendy Matheka. https://www.wendymatheka.com/post/journal-prompts-for-inner-child-healing

McBride Sr, C. (2023, May 2). Addressing Emotional Wounds: The Hidden Key to Success and Well-Being. Www.linkedin.com. https://www.linkedin.com/pulse/addressing-emotional-wounds-hidden-key-success-christopher-mcbride-sr/

Morin, A. (2023, May 9). How Cognitive Reframing Works. Verywell Mind. https://www.verywellmind.com/reframing-defined-2610419

Neff, K. (2015). Self-Compassion. Self-Compassion. https://self-compassion.org/

Ola, F. (2024, December 26). 100+ Shadow Work Journal Prompts for Healing and Self Discovery. Her Lifestyle Pursuit. https://herlifestylepursuit.com/shadow-work-journal-prompts/

O'Connell, R. (2023, June 1). The Importance of Overcoming Limiting Beliefs (With Examples) | Guider AI. Guider-Ai.com. https://guider-ai.com/blog/overcoming-limiting-beliefs/

Pedneault, K. S. (n.d.). How Accepting Difficult Emotions Can Improve Emotional Health. Very Well Mind. https://www.verywellmind.com/how-accepting-emotions-can-improve-emotional-health-425368#toc-why-accepting-emotions-is-helpful

Penrose, C. (2024, November 13). 50 Shadow Self Journal Prompts. LeStallion. https://lestallion.com/blogs/journal-prompts/50-shadow-self-journal-prompts?srsltid=AfmBOoqhoxUyOUWxdb8uLqAEMeZQmPDrkNA4HpifL6ZSek8WhN-P6-YH

Perry, E. (2022, June 13). 8 Benefits of Shadow Work and How to Start Practicing It. Www.betterup.com. https://www.betterup.com/blog/shadow-work

Perry, E. (2024, February 28). 75 Shadow Work Prompts for Healing, Growth, & Mental Health. Www.betterup.com. https://www.betterup.com/blog/shadow-work-prompts

Psychologs Magazine. (2023, May 16). Carl Jung's Concept of Individuation. Psychologs Magazine | Mental Health Magazine | Psychology Magazine | Self-Help Magazine. https://www.psychologs.com/carl-jungs-concept-of-individuation/?srsltid=AfmBOoqW8ZUALVehRc638r3bBk08f_Yq1GDaVQwOqXbtAfePwzGZj1M0

Raypole, C. (2021, May 17). Ready, Set, Journal! 64 Journaling Prompts for Self-Discovery. Psych Central. https://psychcentral.com/blog/ready-set-journal-64-journaling-prompts-for-self-discovery#the-journal-prompts

Recognizing and Coping with Negative Emotions. (n.d.). www.hopkinsmedicine.org. https://www.hopkinsmedicine.org/about/community-health/johns-hopkins-bayview/services/called-to-care/recognize-cope-with-negative-emotions

Resnick, A. (2024, December 6). 25 Questions to Help You Discover Your True Passions. Very Well Mind. https://www.verywellmind.com/25-questions-to-discover-your-passions-8754230

Roy, M. (2024, March 12). 3 Lessons from Brené Brown that Will Help You Embrace Your Authenticity. Medium. https://medium.com/@roymihika06/3-lessons-from-bren%C3%A9-brown-that-will-help-you-embrace-your-authenticity-8910d8d28471

Sandstone Care Team. (2025, February 5). Journal Prompts for Mental Health: Boost Your Well-Being. Sandstone Care. https://www.sandstonecare.com/blog/journal-prompts-mental-health/

Sargeant, K. (n.d.). Getting to Know Your Shadow. The Tools. https://www.thetoolsbook.com/blog/getting-to-know-your-shadow

Saxena, M. (2024, April 26). Self-Integration: 5 Key Principles. Linkedin.com. https://www.linkedin.com/pulse/self-integration-5-key-principles-manasi-saxena-xhdcc/

Schlamm, L. (2014). Individuation. Encyclopedia of Psychology and Religion, 866–870. https://doi.org/10.1007/978-1-4614-6086-2_329

Schroeder, W. (2023, August 23). Somatic Experiencing (SE): Understanding Dr. Peter Levine's Trauma Therapy – Just Mind. Just Mind. https://justmind.org/somatic-experiencing-se-understanding-dr-peter-levines-trauma-therapy/

Sciandra, F. (2019, August 15). 30 Journal Prompts to Explore Your Creativity, Desires, and Passions. Francesca Sciandra. https://francescasciandra.com/blog/30-journal-prompts-to-explore-your-creativity-desires-and-passions

Simone. (2023, March 7). 75 Powerful Journal Prompts For Forgiveness. We Mind Growth. https://wemindgrowth.com/journal-prompts-for-forgiveness/#15-selfforgiveness-journal-prompts

Sonia. (2022, February 5). How Did I Overcome My Limiting Beliefs through Journaling. Aligned Business Alchemy. https://soniamotwani.com/journaling-through-limiting-beliefs/

Starfire, A. L. (2017, May 8). 6 Journaling Prompts to Conquer Your Inner Critic – Writing Through Life. Writingthroughlife.com. https://writingthroughlife.com/6-journaling-prompts-to-conquer-your-inner-critic/

TalktoAngel . (2024, December 20). Online Counselling | Online Therapy| Marriage Counsellors | TalktoAngel. TalktoAngel. https://www.talktoangel.com/blog/understanding-emotional-blocks-causes-symptoms-and-solutions

Team Asana. (2021, November 29). 10 limiting beliefs and how to overcome them. Asana. https://asana.com/resources/limiting-beliefs

Van, H. (2023, August 9). Limiting Beliefs: How They Hold You Back and How to Break Free. Day One | Your Journal for Life. https://dayoneapp.com/blog/limiting-beliefs/#h-journal-prompts-for-identifying-and-challenging-limiting-beliefs

Villines, Z. (2022, August 30). What is shadow work? Benefits and exercises. Www.medicalnewstoday.com. https://www.medicalnewstoday.com/articles/what-is-shadow-work#benefits

What is Individuation? Carl Jung and the Journey of Self. (2018, March 22). Harley TherapyTM Blog. https://www.harleytherapy.co.uk/counselling/what-is-individuation-carl-jung.htm

Wooll, M. (2022, July 19). Don't let limiting beliefs hold you back. Learn to overcome yours. BetterUp. https://www.betterup.com/blog/what-are-limiting-beliefs

Your "Shadow" Self – What It Is, And How It Can Help You. (2017, September 7). Harley TherapyTM Blog. https://www.harleytherapy.co.uk/counselling/shadow-self.htm

Image Sources

1 Photo by James Wheeler: https://www.pexels.com/photo/silhouette-of-person-standing-on-bridge-414523/

2 Photo by Arina Krasnikova: https://www.pexels.com/photo/a-woman-in-knit-sweater-hugging-self-5709914/

3 Photo by Pixabay: https://www.pexels.com/photo/lonely-girl-sitting-on-a-doorway-236215/

4 Photo by Brett Sayles: https://www.pexels.com/photo/grayscale-photo-of-man-thinking-in-front-of-analog-wall-clock-1194196/

5 Photo by Andrea Piacquadio: https://www.pexels.com/photo/photo-of-woman-looking-at-the-mirror-774866/

6 Photo by Serkan Göktay: https://www.pexels.com/photo/woman-standing-near-body-of-water-66758/

www.ingramcontent.com/pod-product-compliance
Lightning Source LLC
Chambersburg PA
CBHW051850160426
43209CB00006B/1235